Life....

Life....

THROUGH THE EYES OF A STRANGER

Stacy Hortaridis

authorHOUSE®

AuthorHouse™
1663 Liberty Drive
Bloomington, IN 47403
www.authorhouse.com
Phone: 1-800-839-8640

First published by AuthorHouse   06/23/2011

ISBN: 978-1-4634-2331-5 (sc)
ISBN: 978-1-4634-2341-4 (ebk)

Library of Congress Control Number: 2011909803

Printed in the United States of America

Any people depicted in stock imagery provided by Thinkstock are models, and such images are being used for illustrative purposes only.
Certain stock imagery © Thinkstock.

This book is printed on acid-free paper.

Because of the dynamic nature of the Internet, any web addresses or links contained in this book may have changed since publication and may no longer be valid. The views expressed in this work are solely those of the author and do not necessarily reflect the views of the publisher, and the publisher hereby disclaims any responsibility for them.

Illustrated by James Hortaridis

In loving memory of my father . . .
We love and miss you.

Tears are like shadows
Always wanting to hide.
We know that they're there
They come from inside.

We keep them locked up
Till dark, when they're seen
Only the heavens
Can say what they mean.

Though shadows are empty
But not so the heart;
Tears are to help us
To tell them apart.

Stacy Hortaridis

How much of illusion
We shall be able to say
Once to cover the eyes
Has come to end this day

Never question how it's there
Never question when to end
For always in the heart
Forever in life a friend

Feelings of illusion
Slowly pass and fade
We learn that our reality
Is only what we've made?

Being happy where we stand
Never fearing, how far, to fall
For if we ever do
It'll be worth it all

With roads all around
We've been times before
As people draw near
Will we just slam the door?

When will they open?
What will we see?
Will we try to hold on
To what will never be?

In hope of having
The feel of needing
To what extent
Are we exceeding?

To believe in life
And why it is here
To really find out
Who is to dare?

Wondrous illusion
Surrounded conclusion
Wanting to be enfolded
Into what we have scolded

Needing what was more
Never being sure
For a challenge taken
Could be mistaken

With fun, in search of truth
All but forgotten in youth
Finally come to embrace
The tender-loving face

Through eyes lacking doubt
Forgetting the world about
Wanting to take a chance
And hope for love and romance

Sometimes I sit and think
Feeling as if I want to cry.
I feel so empty inside
And am so confused to why

I don't feel the hurt
But I do feel depressed.
As though my darkest secrets
Are too far suppressed.

Sometimes it gets so bad
That nothing seems to matter.
My soul is lost and confused
As if it were to shatter.

It's hard to hold back the tears
I just have to let them flow.
I try to keep them inside
So no one else will know.

So all I can do is write
To let these feelings go.
Someday I'll know why
These feelings want to show.

Forgiving those
Already forgiven.
When do we stop
Who is forbidden?

Lovers of friends
To draw the line
To know the difference
Of something too fine

To know the truth
Challenge the lies
Can it always be read
In the others' eyes?

Why can't it be said?
Why all the games?
Not to put love
With labels or names.

Afraid to be shown
But why only fear?
We've already seen
With more than one tear.

With empty thoughts
Within the night
The caress of peace
An empty sight

We hope to dream
Of days gone past,
To the happy times
We thought would last.

We know they're there
Only harder to find,
With all of the pressure
We put on our mind.

To keep the peace
The emptiness to fill
We dream of hope
And someday we will.

Love engulfed heart and mind.
Is it in truth he is so kind?
The words expressed to really show
That of the heart we already know.
In blindness of mind we are not clear.
The questions to ask, we do not dare.
The answers we find may only confuse
What we in life are afraid to lose.
Walls we've built, never to fall
May come down after all.
Wanting to be free to fly.
Not held down with only a cry.
It has to be felt from deep within.
If only to please, could end in sin.
For hurt in the other, never forgot
To rethink the lesson life has taught.
To know the love is of heart and mind.
To know in truth, he is so kind.

Where is the love
He is to show?
Only in words
Never to know.

It has been said
That it is in truth.
But we are no longer
As we were in our youth.

Forgetting the freedom
And a piece of the heart
We held for the love
We hoped life would start.

So must we hold on
To what we believed?
There is always love
For our heart to conceive.

What is inside?
I've no way to know.
Where does it come from?
Where does it go?

It left for a while
Now it is here.
What does it want?
What does it fear?

The tears or the pain?
Or what I can't find?
How can we answer
To what we are blind?

To fear only love
For what can it mend?
To someday believe
Our heart is our friend.

Was there ever a time . . .
You thought no one cared?
Those who said they did
Are now running scared.

They were there in the beginning.
Said they'd stay till the end.
But all of a sudden one day,
They're no longer your friend.

At first they were supportive
But now they're walking away.
Could people be so cruel?
To leave, with nothing to say?

Was there ever a time . . .
You felt so scared
Because at one time
They said that they cared?

When I'm sitting alone
Thinking all night.
Looking out my window
Feeling a little fright.

Watching the leaves
As the wind would blow
A lonely feeling
Would run through my soul.

I'd feel really weird
Like a lonely bird in the sky
I'd keep looking around
And wondering why?

Why are things the way they are?
Why do they have to go so far?
So far down where I can't let it go.
How to lose it, I just don't know.

Life is full of surprises.
Just when you've figured them out,
God decides to be humorous
And knocks you all about.

To give your life a twirl
And something new to decide
With so many roads and choices,
It's his humor we use as our guide.

Because we don't hear his laughter
We know not of his wit.
And though we're pushed to limits
We know we'll never quit.

In snow-filled skies
One bird as he flies
Through the silence of dust,
Knowing he must.

To complete his flight
As the world turns to night
From the skies now black
He sees what we lack.

The grace of his world
From a heart full of love
For seeing our world
From his up above.

Confusion Complete

The emptiness complete
The void is now surrounded
Is it with complication of time
Or was the love never really founded

But why could the loss of one
then lead to three
Why is the only one left
Left there with only me

Is this what there is
Or can it be made to change
As I see it all before me
Waiting to rearrange

Is hope all, on which, I can depend
What will be when that's taken away
Am I the one taking too much?
Who is left to really say?

For now I'm completely alone
With nowhere left to fall
With no direction to land
Is it hopeless after all?

Looking Past the Beginning

What of life is left to give
What of life is left to take
When confusion is so self-surrounded
There's nothing more of it to make

To be so self-surrounded
That the mind must forget
To feel the feelings its had
Even if one's ways are set

To hold inside the pain and anger
How do I learn to let myself out?
Who will be there, and listening?
When it's my turn to scream and shout

I have to learn to be self-dependent
When the answers I cannot find
From deep within the heart
I have to follow my own mind

We live each day
For reasons unknown
In this circle of life
What are we shown?

Confusion of love
Feelings of hate
For the simple fact
We can't cheat fate.

Though we try and we fail
And choose, as we will
The roads that we travel
Seem emptier still.

Each day that we live
Often we wonder
If these feelings of fear,
Would put us asunder?

Lonely For Love

This feeling is taking over again
Sometimes life just isn't fair
When you really need your friends
It seems they just don't care

My best friend isn't here for me
And I have no boyfriend to hold
So I'll have to deal with this myself
Which may turn my heart very cold

Though I can't really blame them
For it was I who made this be
I wouldn't trust anyone enough
To show them what's deep inside of me

I can't expect them to try and help
When I myself won't even try
As I look around at my loneliness
I hold back my tears with a sigh

I have this hollow emptiness inside
But not a feeling by which I abide
As if I'm out looking in
A different person of new existence
Maybe a hollow heart with more resistance
Maybe not of heart, but of broader mind
Even if it's broader, can the heart be kind
I know how to put feelings where they belong
So maybe I'm finally learning to be strong
Though life's lesson is not one of power
We certainly were not meant to cower
So what of life's game do we partake
What of our emotional status do we make
Were we meant to be cruel or to be kind
Or do we walk, felling empty and blind
If you are kind—life may not be as you choose
For there is more cruelness, you may feel as you lose
But do we really lose out in the end
For we who are kind, we do have a friend
When it seems loneliness is the only one
Someone comes along and shows you the sun
Thought at first it may not seem as bright
With each step of trust you will see the light

Feelings so strong
What do they lack
To be where I was,
How to get back

What is the void
Can't say, unknown
What emptiness is
What light isn't shown

To turn it on
Would it fill
The hole inside
Or is it by will

The will to love
The will to live
How can I take
What others won't give

Your world is your kingdom
Where you sit on your throne
You sometimes feel empty
Lost and alone

A world you've divided
You now try to mend
When you bring it together
I hope there's a friend

For in a world of confusion
To find peace of mind
We all need someone
In our lives to be kind

Stacy Hortaridis

Everyone wants to know
People can only guess
When building on ones life
And finding only a mess

Who's to say they're right
Who's to say I'm wrong
You can't tell me where to fit
I can't find where I belong

Just because words are different
The meanings are the same
People trying to come in
But it's all just a game

So our lives we spend in question
The answers are lost in space
And every day that we live
We hope we can find our place

Time To Love?

With all that I feel in my heart,
When do I learn to start?
To deal with the weakness and pain
And not to think him so vain

Because it feels right, is it wrong
Can showing weakness be strong?
But why to love do we fear
And at the thought shed a tear?

We've cried from the anger and hate
And the walls are all a part of fate
But to uncover what is behind
Can we really settle the mind?

To believe every word that's spoken
And take it to heart as a token
Of the love and trust we've built
To finally let go, without guilt

Have I found such truth
Or is the heart again blind
To answer such questions
We must look beyond the mind

How did I get where I don't belong
To put me there to prove that I'm strong
If weakness can provide togetherness
But letting go, whom would it distress
To a point where we can always refrain
And in our own feeling, we will remain
Is it just a game we all play?
To believe me in all that I say
With life being so obscure
Who are the ones to cure?
But is there really anything behind
To what we disagree can only be of mind
Then togetherness becomes departure
From feelings we were never too sure

Departure is the one to rule
Am I again, the fool?
I guess wanting and believing
Are the differences between getting and receiving

In wanting do we choose not to believe
To make it easier to retrieve
Then is it forever gone?
Does that make it wrong?

But in love what is right
With ourselves we only fight
To believe in what we want
But our doubt will always haunt

Do we let the desire lie
And on loneliness are we high
All to do is bear it and sigh
For always, we say goodbye!

From where they stand do they see
Who, and of what may be
Can we forget and just go on
But what with patience can be too long
Knowing they don't understand
But who is the one to reprimand
Not knowing ignorance from defeat
To what middle do we choose to meet
Denying admittance to what we defy
From which point do we decide to try
To accept what there is inside
By which of the two to confide
Only silence can defeat defiance
Who is the one to show compliance?

All the lies—to begin truth
Did they all start in youth?
But why the need to hide
In truth, have they tried?

When did it leave, where did it go
I guess in reality, I'll never know
But to analyze how it became
Does it all end up the same

Or with anger, in many layers
For all who are the betrayers
Are they really in a world their own?
For their lack of feelings to be shown

It is all just to excite
In life what might

But why hold on to the past
The one thing to always last

For something that was taken away
I guess I will never be one to say

Being what we want
Seeing what we hate
Living how we are
Who is to debate?

No one can be right
Life is only wrong
To expect so much
From one not too strong

Where does strength begin?
Or is it all just a game
No matter how good it is
It all ends up the same

Loneliness comes with pain
And at what cost do we pay
What reality is to happiness?
The day we pass away?

Then our souls are free!

With love in the mind
The heart to beware
Is the game in motion?
Or could he really care

For what or for whom
Why do I believe?
Is it now me
Who'll learn to retrieve?

Who choose now?
Why within him
Is it going to prove
Only within sin

To feel the strength
And fear the weak
What from him
Is it I seek?

Will time only tell
That I'm only a fool
And that my weakness
Is only his tool?

There are no dreams to be dreamt
There is no love found or lost
What is the emptiness that lies?
When upon the wind, is it tossed?

Within words that are spoken
But none too deep to be heard
Though we know not what lies within
Where do we choose to be lured

Will honesty someday fulfill
What we in our lives deny
So what is felt till that day
That we break our barrier and try

To dream the impossible
To feel only the wanted
And leave behind us
Our pasts for the haunted

Love to be given
Love to be taken
We're always the ones
So easily mistaken

Always a fool
Breaking the rule
Believing what's not
A lesson untaught

How to be rid of
Something we've fought
Want of the love
Always to be sought

Who to accept
Who to be lost
No matter the price
Forget the cost

Everyone else does
So why not I
If they don't,
Why even try

Love is a battle
And who is at war
Who is to fool
Who is to score

Hearts given easily
Only a fool will say
Those who keep fighting
In the end will pay

For what the costs
And who's to decide
Which road to choose
What law to abide

Laws of the heart
Laws of the mind
How patient to be
To what we will find

Who is to care
Who is to know
To believe in the war
The love wants to show

Friends are in circles
Supposing never to end
But what with those
Whose lives never mend

So broken and fragile
When am I to be free
Of the pain and anguish
Forever haunting me

Will love of life
Or life of love
Help me escape
To rise above

Where do we go?
Where do we soar?
When hope's too high
It's crushed to the floor

To pick ourselves up
How many times must we try
And, for what reason, believe
They'll never say goodbye

Feeling there's no end
Searching for a friend
Not knowing where to look
Or the feeling that it shook
For friends in love
Always feeling above
Why is their heart so cold
What secrets lie untold
With weakness of the mind
Who is left to be kind
Playing life's cruel game
Am I ever to claim fame
To be as they are
Play the game too far
How shallow could happiness be
From what point do they see
To accept no challenge, make no change
Has the emptiness, to them, ever felt strange
Have they ever analyzed their being
And hated, before them, what they are seeing
For can I only witness the guilt
For in turn, the walls we built
Why do we always run and hide
Can I only welcome myself to sit by my side

I know where you are
I've been there before
You feel all alone
And very unsure

Believe in your strength
And take it day by day
Listen to your heart
And what it has to say

It can help you through times
When all you need is a friend
It shows us how to reach inside
And help ourselves mend

Doing this for yourself
May seem hardest of all
But the strength you have inside
Will carry you over that wall.

Stacy Hortaridis

Fool In Love

As I lie here and think
Thoughts of you on my mind
I never knew sweet memories
Could be so brutal and so unkind

I try to think of good times
But kept asking, "why?"
I try to put the blame on you
But all I can do is cry

You were so tender in your ways
Which always made me smile
But you were different and free
Which made loving you worthwhile

In the long run, I guess I lost
You're the type who needs to be free
I allowed myself to fall in love
I was too much a fool to see

I really thought I could hold on
But it wasn't for too long
Before you were up and gone
Singing that familiar goodbye song

I guess now I must get over you
I'm trying in every possible way
There will be many tears before then
But they'll stop falling some day

I feel I'm falling in love with you
Though I don't want to admit the fact
I don't know if people can notice
So I take caution in how I should act

Though you were somebody else's love
I'm trying to ignore that too
Though she says she doesn't love you
I'm thinking of what I should do

Though it seems I should feel guilt
For what I feel may cause pain
Though I don't even know how you feel
Or if there's anything from this to gain

I'm telling you all that's inside me
When I don't know if you care
I may make a fool of myself
Over feelings we don't even share

It's all happening too fast
Too fast for words to explain
I don't know if I should feel this way
But it's too hard to refrain

I guess there's only one thing left to do
To take things day by day
Please tell me what's going on inside you
I need to hear what you have to say.

Feeling compelled
To know how to trust
The day will come
When I know I must

Thinking too shallow
To wound the heart
To think before speaking
How do I start?

For faith between friends
Is what life needs?
To rid ourselves
Of our foolish greed's

If only the words
Could truly say
How deeply I feel
For thinking that way

The Great Wall

I have many people in my life
But I somehow shy away
And when I'm with each one of them
It's as if I have nothing to say

I feel as I'm someone different
Is it someone else I see?
Someone with more resistance
Why is it so uncomfortable to me

It's like I'm feeling guilty
Though there's no reason for the guilt
It's as though I'm leaning too hard
On these stonewalls I have built

I've realized I'm hiding too deep within
Maybe people should know what I'm about
But who wants to listen and understand
My thoughts, my fears, my doubt

So how do we who are sheltered,
Finally climb over that wall
Do we need to believe in ourselves?
And realize it's the worth the fall?

Love and Life

Something is going on inside him
But I have not the guts to ask
For will I find that the answer
Wasn't worth the task

For me to put my heart on the line
Is something I've done before
But I always end up losing
By a very defeating score

Why can't love be simple
The way is was always meant
So instead of nights of crying
Our time would be better spent

Maybe I should give up the challenge
And find something simple and pure
For maybe then I'll feel the love
But I've never felt it, how can I be sure

New Experiences

When I get in my moods
I sit and ask myself why
Why do I dwell on the past
It only makes me sigh

To know there's so much I could've taken
But merely let it go
Why I foolishly did that
I guess it's too late to know

There was so much love given
All I did was watch it pass by
Why couldn't I return the love
Was it the fact of being shy

Maybe just plain scared
But what was there to fear
The thought of being loved,
Or the feelings I'd be forced to share

I Cry Now

I feel my heart and soul cry
Not for the present, but past
For things I have done
And have happened to me
Because I didn't cry then . . .
I cry now

For people I've lost
People I've hurt and me
For the loneliness brought pain
Too far suppressed . . .
I cry now

For things I've learned
But wish I didn't
But glad I did
To teach others
Things that were taken away
Much, much too soon . . . .

I cry now!

Maybe the people will change
And faces may fade
But do the feelings change
For each friend we've made

Circumstances may change, as do crowds
And with each flow brings the unforeseen
Are we ready to face this challenge
To take time to find what it may mean

Can people bring together a closeness
That is rare, but could be bound
Can they share their minds and souls
Could something like this be found

Could they take the challenge together
And bare the darkness and pain
If they expand within themselves
And, on the outside, need not explain?

What Truth To Life

Life is so very different
Looking from the inside
No longer bound to my walls
Not living in a world to divide

The pain from the emptiness
But where is all the shame?
Is it locked within the walls?
A part of me I've come to tame

With confidence in awareness
What part has come to truce?
To be what is, yet what's not
Which of the two was let loose

What I want, what I dream
What I hate, what I defy
Have I lived to see
All I wished to deny?

In a world full of hate
In a world full of love
Which of these two
Do I wish to be above

Can there be any more
Or just what there is
But who is by my side
Who is to really care?

Me?
See:
Love is an illusion
We play on our mind
The soul can be meaning
But the heart to be kind?
Is there such truth?

Trying To Be My Own

When put in life to find a maze
Do we then forget to put aside haze?
Do clouds creep in and slowly contort
What we, ourselves, find hard to sort
When things are taken for what they're said
When do we believe the words we are fed?
With people so complex, we can't figure out
If what's said is real, that's why there's doubt
To stand where we have—afraid to fall
Is it weakness that tells us what's not at all?
When must we learn to look beyond truth?
And trust in love, as we did in our youth
When one's trust is not easy to confide
The feelings we have, how to put them aside
When to keep hold, when to let go of
But what to be done with uncontained love
How are we careful in feeling too free
Is that when we refrain, or just let be
How can it be, when I tend to seek
In others, believing there's a cold streak
Should I look at myself, maybe others see
What I seek in others, do they seek of me?

Dividing The Wall

Why do I feel as encircled
I feel, as I must stand-alone
But even with people surrounded
I'm the emptiest person I've known

With emptiness so completely filled
To scramble and confuse the mind
How can I in both body and soul
Be persistent and yet be kind

Though alone, I have been before
I dealt with it then, so why is it now
It seems almost impossible to learn
Are the stakes too high to master somehow

Even though it goes much higher
Who's to say that the walls are not
When to come down, layer by layer,
To find the things we have sought

If the questions are self-seeking
How are we clear and unconfused
What to be of the unprotected heart
Is it then that we feel we are used

Fighting Dependence

Here I sit in the dark
I'm as alone as I shall be
As the silence now surrounds
Who is it to set me free?

What is to come of independence
It is self-sought or misunderstood
Because everyone's listening not hearing
Or just that I thought they would

Am I a prisoner of my own walls
In not being where I belong?
Who am I fighting to get out?
The one who believes I'm wrong

Who's left to say I'm right
Must I, in turn, be the judge
To look around at what I have
And to those, hold no grudge

With past forgotten, fears remain
Was it I who brought me here?
Because I'm the one remaining
What will be of what's not there?

Should it remain unwanted
Or become more fought for
When do the pieces all fit?
When I myself am not sure

Growing Pains

The words are always the same
Maybe I'm imagining it's me
So how can I be ignorant
To something I can't even see

Why is it always to be hidden
Not too easily misunderstood
I'm reaching too far to the future
The past crawls out from the woods

That is what makes us unhappy
For the mistakes we will always pay
And yet to face them beforehand
You will listen and hear what they say

So when do we allow ourselves to realize
The thin line has been finely crossed
With confusion so completely there
Do we then also realize—we're lost

Hidden Fears

If I were able to, just once
Open up and say what I think
Who would then be laughing
Would my heart, then again sink

When is it real and how is it known
When we don't admit to feel the same
Will no one open up for the fear
Of the past they've had in shame

Why must it always be so
That we live for what we've done
Must we feel a need to explain
Where does it end and new life begun

Is it when those are brought to face
What of when the fears run too deep
Do the lies become too far hidden
To trust anyone, with them, to keep

With another secret now revealed
And all the years of self-concealed
What of the walls I have built
Why is it always love with guilt
Can these secrets set my soul
Will it be gain of self-control
What of the shame and dirt be felt
With many of losses under my belt
Losses of love, losses of pride
Do I welcome myself to sit by my side
Is it not impossible for me to be "I"?
To not ask too much, the question of why
For need of the future, with memory of the past
We can take into learning, the things we have grasped
No matter with life, in good or bad
We all have the need, and right, to be sad
To feel and grieve, for what we have the need
Who is to say it's done only for greed
For we who give, do not in turn take
For we stand alone, for ourselves, our sake
With misunderstanding, not as my guide
To see it alright to sit by my side

Living To Learn—Learning To Live

With the way life is now
To survive, tell me how
When someone can step in and grab hold
And it's your life they begin to mold
Not caring who it might hurt
Digging up the already buried dirt
How can one individual continue to live
When life throws back everything that you give
For in learning to control my own
Thinking in soul, I've truly grown
They now think the soul can be sold
Who then, will learn of the secrets untold
What's said, and with the hatred be done
Which of us will be the first to run
Who's life will be miserable and distraught
And all for a lesson life's already taught

The Inner Power

No matter how free the soul is
Or how high it wants to soar
There's always something in the way
Slamming that halfway open door

Wondering if I'm never to come out
Of the fantasy web, which I weave
With people running in and out
Who will stay? Who will leave?

Do I expect them to be stronger
And accept the games I play
Though they do come from reason
A part of my life, they do portray

Though test could complete failure
Which some try to reprehend
Should the wall finally come down?
Then will it be I to commend

Can there be any in between found?
Is there such a half built wall?
Maybe I do expect them to be stronger
For I feel that I am not at all

Only In Emptiness

Knowing what you're going through
Cause you've been that road before
You always thought you were stronger
But now with old ways, you're not sure

With all the love around
There is never love of one
With strength, only in mind
The confusion has finally begun

Why in strength is there emptiness
With such loneliness, we tend to fear
For what we look for, or what we find
Do we look back on strength to bear?

In knowing mistrust, do we still believe
In what we fought not to admit
What we so often dream but seldom feel
Do we allow our feelings, then, to commit?

Do we look to pass or freeze
Which has no fear involved
To subject to a life of emptiness
Or in the fear of being dissolved

Why is it no one thinks as I
And without need to analyze
Am I more insecure or blind
To what they know, I wont realize

But in knowing as they do
How do I learn the lesson they've taught
And stop looking for the past
With all the feelings I have fought

Am I that afraid to open my eyes
To what will be there, or what won't
Every time I start to trust
Something inside screams out, "don't"

How do I stop the judgment
When fear is the much stronger
Will confidence be the only one
To say insecure will be no longer

Why In Him

Being in a world of unseen
Within words we became friends
But only in a way so complex
What are the secrets he defends

Asking only what I understand
The words become only a thought
Some, for which, are misunderstood
But in him I find fear that is not

In such a concrete, complex way
That we can't keep the secrets aside
Have we now come to the wall's end?
Forget what we valued with pride

For the lessons are only lies
In an insecure way we know
But not to let ourselves out
With true feelings not to show

Are all forgotten, but too soon
Is there such a total trust
Which, would only make us part
So only in believing we must.

Too much confusion
Nothing is clear
Can it be done
If only in fear

Running to walls
Without any end
Does life believe
Not to have friends

His life's complete
Without a doubt
When to stand up
To learn how to shout

No one will listen
No one will hear
How can I, alone
Be one to bear

How much to take
Before we fall
When do we stop
Walking to walls

You once said you loved me
But nothing came to face
As in trying to let go
With some respectful grace

Words of illusion
To never fully replace
The love that comes from the heart
When you see your child's face

To think of ones self
Choosing to leave it behind
Can it only be that easy
For a love so hard to find

Not knowing where you stand
Or what it is you choose
For a love so deeply felt
Is it worth the risk to lose?

Putting It Together

I'm holding the final pieces
Now will they complete as one
Now that the pain has surfaced
What is there left to be done?

But what became of the anger
I never felt it leave
Is it what I must be ignorant to
Or something I must retrieve?

Why can't I overcome the love
Why can't the hate overrule
Is it more the pity I feel
That allowed me to love one so cruel

Why does he refuse to let go?
Is it that he's really trying to hide?
Or am I the one who's being blinded
To what's really going on inside?

A Lesson To Learn

Now with no more questions
Is there a lesson I have learned
Now maybe I can go after
The things that I have yearned

With love right within my grasp
Will my faith in love now return
Do I go in with my eyes open wide
Or open minded with no concern

Not to think of what will be lost
But to think of what will be gained
When love is what I feel inside
My hearts not too easily refrained

Somehow now it feels different
For him I feel I can trust
To remember to be careful
Is something I feel I must.

With the person, I think he is
Is it him I've been waiting for?
How do I learn to open my heart?
To open that once closed door

I guess I must remember that lesson
One, which is very seldom taught
To learn how to accept the love
And forget the fears I've fought

Well the answers are found
And it's just what I thought
Love is never real
Just a lesson to be taught

We learn of the hardness
We learn of the coldness
One we don't learn
Is the lesson of boldness

Always afraid to feel
Wondering if we have the right
To take someone's heart
And treat it as we might

I guess I was taught my lesson
Of never again to be the fool
Though you think love is real
Yet you learn it's only cruel

Chris

You've told me you loved me
And I know it's what you feel
But my feelings aren't as strong
For me, love may never be real

For I know you are sincere
And I want you as a friend
But this is not my time
My heart needs time to mend

I'm young with a sense of freedom
But you're looking to settle down
I have too many years ahead of me
So upon that notion I do frown

You have very different ideas of love
It's not something, in which, I believe
It's something I've given out before
But never in return have received

I know you've been hurt in the past
But now you can look past the pain
My heart is still cold to the feeling of love
I still can't see, what from it, you gain

I want to walk away from this, you my friend
I don't want to hurt you in any way
But our feelings toward each other differ
And this, there's no easy way to say

Elliot

The mind too complex
To answer the heart
If they would help
I'd love to start

To help you understand
I don't think I could
To end what I started
I did what I should

Though at times it is empty
But this is a must
To be with myself
Before I can trust

To know what I feel
Is mine to be felt
Always learning too late
Is what I was dealt

Now to handle the guilt
Of knowing the pain
To believe what I did
Was not done in vain.

Joe

With eyes so true
Love too pure
Only on that
I am sure

Feelings in deep
Never to fear
The smile
Of only one tear

Forever forgotten
Never mislead
Only the dreams
Of today, instead

Only in love
Can one grow . . .
Never buried
Under the snow

Stacy Hortaridis

Seeing death on the horizon
Within the setting sun
The peaceful flow of water
Loneliness to overcome

The emptiness too hollow
To hear the rush of the waves
Hidden in the dunes,
Built around life's caves.

Happiness lost forever
In the darkness of the light
Like stars against the sky
So beautiful to the sight

So why when they fall do we wish
Upon their death to come true
The happiness that we lost
As they fall to the ocean so blue.

With the wind only a whisper
The whispers only a shriek
When do they come to end
At what forbidden peak?

Shall the two come together?
Can they never learn to shout?
As within the world of a storm
Only one secret that life's about

Only happiness to keep calm
The storms of a loving sea
For the hatred to lie within
The whispers of love shall be

To calm the heart of the wind
As she settles down to sleep
Always to hold with her
The whispers she shall keep

The forest grows wide
The ocean so deep
The tides as they turn
The animals, they sleep

The stars as they float
Through the glow of the moon
The sun as she sleeps
Will awaken, too soon

And all that is silent
Will come from the bliss
And give to the moon
Our dreams we will miss

Though their world is ours
There life's so serene
What they have awake,
Can we only dream?

The rain as it beats
The air seems still
The clouds as they empty
The dreams that they fill

Dreams of the water
As it falls from the sky
The moon as she struggles
From the clouds to get by

To quiet the dreams
With a peaceful glow
To bring back the sounds
Of the night as we know.

The stars light the sky
Like thoughts in a dream
When the sun is awaken
Will she say what they mean?

For who knows the answers
To our dreams where we hide
We wait for the morning
To sit by our side

To feel only warmth
Till you settle to sleep
To bring back the stars
My heart wants to keep

That one fallen star
With a kiss and a prayer
In hopes to be strong
And show that we care

Virgin Islands

The sun as she sets
Behind the hills
The moon as she brightens
The darkness she fills

The land so beautiful
A sight to the eye
As we settle to sleep
With the ease of a sigh

A world left behind
Not soon to forget
Leaving for home
With not one regret

The memories now settle
To a place of their own
For a wonderful land
To many, called home

Stacy Hortaridis

Family is love
We all need to know.
Feeling surrounded
A feeling to show.

To know you're needed
By people who care
Who'll always in life
Be there to share.

The joy and the pain
Of life's ups and downs
To bring up the hopes
Of smiles turned to frowns

Don't ever let go
Of family held dear
In good times and bad
They'll always be near.

Stacy Hortaridis

Mom and Dad

Life is a journey
That you've traveled well
With bumps and bruises
As each of us fell

You picked us back up
And pushed us along
Doing what was right
When we thought you were wrong

You gave us your wisdom
And the love that we need
To pass to our children
On this they will feed

How to repay you
When life's not that long
But the feelings of love
Will always be strong

My Mother

You are the mother:

Who taught me right from wrong
Who was there to catch me when I fell
To whom I look for comfort when I'm ill
Who in the past, I've blamed my mistakes
But you always understood

You are the friend:

When I was going through rebellion
I'd always wanted to find
I look to for advice, when my life is confused
I look to for comfort when my life is at a low
Who I ask for opinions
For I know yours is honest
Who I can trust with my secrets
For I know you will be silent . . . .
Who I love very much

My Brother

You're someone that I want to know
Though I'm not always apt to show.

You're so reserved it's hard to see
The person inside you've come to be.

You've accomplished a lot through the years
You've felt the pain and maybe the tears.

Be proud of who you are, you've come to shine
As brothers go, I'm glad you're mine.

My Sister

Knowing where the pain is.
It's seen within your eyes.
Knowing it is emptiness
For deep inside it lies.

When all the answers seem hidden
From yourself you wish to hide.
When all the feelings you have
Get all confused inside.

I wish I could make sense of them.
To help you figure them out.
For the emptiness is lonely
When you don't know what it's about.

Remember you are strong.
This in life you've shown.
Even with people around
You feel you're on your own.

We can only hold you.
Or listen to how you feel.
You're the only person
Who'll allow yourself to heal.

Uncle Charlie

Your heart was full of so much love
Now you've taken it to God above.

You were a special friend and one we hold dear
Your laughter and smile will always bring cheer.

Holding on to the laughter you gave from your heart
The memories we cherish and won't let them part.

I hope you are happy with God at your side
We'll always remember you with Love and Pride.

We know you're leaving your family and home
But we know in our hearts you won't be alone.

Billy

Remembering the child
You once used to be
To look at you now
It's amazing to see

The man you're becoming
As each day goes on
Your heart is pure
Your head is strong

You deserve what life gives you
It wasn't for free
You use God's gifts
To become what you'll be

The choice is yours
To decide what to do
Just always remember
How much we love you.

Cody

With a life so precious,
God wants to give
The opportunity to grow
To prosper, to live

You've had such a struggle.
We knew you'd pull through.
With all of the love,
What else could you do?

We know you'll be with us
For many years to come
You're life's little blessing
A miracle, to some.

So when you get older
You can always say:
"I've been through this much;
nothing can stand in my way."

My Daughter

You're a life so fragile
Just beginning to grow.
To feel nothing unkind
Of the world as we know.

With life so unfair
For a heart so true
You feel only love
For all that you do.

The simplest of pleasure
In a world all your own
From the visions of love
You're constantly shown.

A child is wonder
With a beautiful glow
We fill them with love
And the life that we know

We hope for their future
As each day they grow
We teach them our ways
And hope that they know

Decisions we've made
We've made out of love
And know that we've tried
With strength from above

To do what was best
So you'll know that we care
And these feelings of love
We hope that we'll share.

Ashlie

The aching that I feel
My heart will only endure
For with every step you take
The pride shows that much more

Wanting to hold on
Know only to try
To pick you up when you fall
To hold you when you cry

To lessen the pain of life
I'd do anything if I could
To keep you from the hurt
But it will find you, as it would

Only to be there and listen
As my mother did for me
I want us to be friends
Someday we shall be

My love (Raechelle)

The love I feel for her
Is still deep in my soul
The tears I have begun
To keep under control

With the pain still real
And the love still strong
Will the fear of memory
Make it prolong

Do we know when that may be
Or in time, ever find
Or will the heart be guided
By the place that's always blind

Never to forget the agony
Or to remember the joy
Of what she would've brought
Like a brand new baby toy

So full of needs and wants
And of two, be me
But another time in life
God will let that be.

The holiday nearing
What will it bring?
Will the heart be sagging?
Or at last will it sing?

To the holiday songs
We hear every year,
To give to my child
That holiday cheer.

To finally look past
The sorrow and pain.
To remember in life
The ones that I've gained

A Child's Christmas

Her eyes light up
With a beautiful glow
From all of the trimmings
Of Christmas we know.

A heart full of wonder
And the holiday cheer
As the season's upon us
And the promise draws near.

The promise of presents
From under the tree
On Christmas morning
From her eyes we'll see.

A wonder of life
So sweet and pure
From a child of love
So fragile and sure.

Stacy Hortaridis

The holiday feeling
Is one of cheer,
Though some of us wish
It would never get here.

The smile of a child
We need to hold dear
To let us forget
Our worries and fears

To see in their eyes
The joy that we miss
When they show us their love
With one single kiss.

Nicholas

Babies are wondrous
A bundle of joy
God's little gift
A girl or a boy

The gift we received
Came bundled in blue
The color of love
That he'll give to you

To brighten our world
With his happy glow
And fill our life
As each day he grows.

Stacy Hortaridis

Friends are for life
Forever held dear.
To give us the smiles
From all that we fear.

Though we've had all the good
Survived all the bad,
I hope in our friendship
You'll never be sad.

Be glad who you are
Be glad who you meet
Don't ever let anyone
Lead you to defeat.

You're special in life
Forever you'll grow.
Remember our friendship
Where ever you go.

Our Friendship

From the first time we met
Understanding and trust had started
As the days went by
We knew we'd never be parted

We knew our friendship was special
As the months rolled into years
We knew the trust was real
When we shared our darkest fears

When people met us for the first time
They always seem to remember our name
Because we don't "act" different
We always "act" the same

People can never figure us out
And don't know what of us to make
We don't try to please anyone
We've taken all that we can take

Special Friend

You live in a world
You think is your own.
Then life takes away
The one thing you've known.

When life's got you feeling
That it never will end.
You feel all alone
Without even one friend.

They're more than you see
In your world where you hide.
If you'd only come out
To let them be by your side.

I wish I could help you
To know people care.
I hope for a friendship,
The two of us can share.

Friend's .... love .... life

I sit now in the shadows and look at my life
I remember where I came from
And where I am now
I remember things I've been through
And what brought me here
I look at where I'm going
And realize how much I've accomplished
How much loneliness there was
And how much I've learned from it
I remember the good and bad times
Which has brought me to appreciate
I'm trying to understand and accept life
And be the best person I can
I guess in searching you need time
And with time brings patience
And patience brings
Friends .... Love .... Life
And in you I found all three